cont

MW00747953

British & North American Readers:
Please note that Australian cup and
spoon measurements are metric. A quick
conversion guide appears on page 63.
A glossary explaining unfamiliar terms
and ingredients begins on page 60.

2 seafood know-how

Many of us shy away from cooking fish and other seafood because we don't know how to prepare it and sometimes we don't know which parts to eat. Here's an easy step-by-step guide.

To remove meat from a cooked crayfish

1. Place crayfish on a board, claws up. Hold the chest flat with one hand and, using a large sharp knife, cut completely through the chest and tail.

2. Turn crayfish around, hold the head flat and cut through the head.

3. Pull the halves apart. Discard the white gills and the grey vein running down the centre back of the tail. The liver is edible although not very attractive. Using your fingers, gently remove the meat from the tail sections.

To remove meat from a cooked crab

1. Hold the crab firmly with one hand and slide a large sharp knife under the top shell at the back. Prise off top shell.

2. Remove and discard the white gills (also called dead men's fingers).

3. Remove and discard the soft spongy innards.

4. Crack claws with a nutcracker or rolling pin; pull meat from the claws with fingers.

To prepare mussels

1. Mussels must be alive when you cook them. Live mussels have tightly closed shells. Look them over and discard any mussels with open shells. Using a sharp, yanking motion, pull away and discard the 'beard', a hairy seaweed growth attached to the mussel shell.

2. Use a kitchen brush to scrub the shells clean under cold running water.

3. Place the mussels in a pan with a spoonful of liquid (water, wine or stock), cover tightly and put over high heat. Check after 2 minutes. Remove any that have opened and return pan to the heat until the remaining mussels open. Discard any that refuse to open. Strain the mussel liquid and keep it to add to the sauce if you're serving one.

To skin a fish fillet

Using a sharp knife, cut a little of the flesh away from the skin at the tail end. Put the fillet on a board, skin-side down, and hold the skin firmly with salted fingers at the tail end. Place the knife flat against the skin and cut the flesh away.

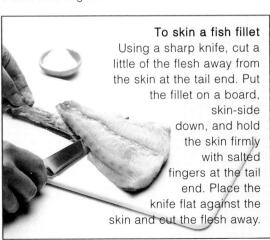

4 spaghetti

with clam sauce

1.5kg fresh clams

1 teaspoon olive oil

2 tablespoons water

1 medium (150g) onion, chopped finely

2 cloves garlic, crushed

2 anchovy fillets, drained, chopped finely

1 small fresh red chilli, seeded, chopped

2 teaspoons chopped fresh thyme

20 medium (1.5kg) egg tomatoes, peeled, seeded, chopped finely

500g spaghetti

2 tablespoons chopped fresh parsley

Cover clams with cold water and soak for 2 hours. Change water twice during soaking.

Heat oil in large pan; add clams, cover with tight-fitting lid. Cook over high heat about 8 minutes or until all clams have opened. Reserve about 10 clams in their shells. Remove remaining clams from shells, discard shells. Strain clam cooking liquid through fine cloth or tea-towel. Return liquid to clean pan, cook, uncovered, until liquid is reduced to 1 cup (250ml).

Combine water, onion, garlic, anchovies, chilli and thyme in large pan; cook, stirring, until onion is soft. Add tomato and reserved clam stock; simmer, uncovered, about 10 minutes, or until sauce is thickened. Add clams and reserved clams in shells; stir until heated through.

Meanwhile, cook pasta in large pan of boiling water, uncovered, until just tender; drain. Serve clam sauce over pasta, sprinkle with parsley.

Microwave Pasta suitable
Per serve fat 3.7g; fibre 12.3g; kj 2279

6 quick **fish**

and prawn curry

Blend or process rind, juice, ginger, garlic, sambal oelek, curry powder and peanuts until smooth.
Shell and devein prawns, leaving heads and tails intact.
Heat large non-stick pan, coat with cooking-oil spray; cook prawns and fish, separately, in batches, until just tender; remove from pan.
Add onion to same pan; cook 1 minute. Add curry mixture, prawns, fish and blended cornflour and water; stir gently over heat until mixture boils and thickens.

½ teaspoon grated lemon rind

⅓ cup (80ml) lemon juice

1 tablespoon grated fresh ginger

2 cloves garlic, peeled

1 teaspoon sambal oelek

2 teaspoons mild curry powder

¼ cup (35g) unsalted roasted peanuts

20 (500g) medium uncooked prawns

cooking-oil spray

4 (800g) boneless white fish fillets, chopped roughly

3 green onions, sliced

2 teaspoons cornflour

¼ cup (60ml) water

Per serve fat 11.6g; fibre 1.4g; kj 1483

barbecued fish with
chilli avocado salsa

We used snapper cutlets for this recipe.

4 (1kg) white fish cutlets

cooking-oil spray

chilli avocado salsa

2 medium (380g) tomatoes, chopped

1 small (200g) avocado, chopped

½ small (40g) onion, chopped

2 tablespoons sweet chilli sauce

1 tablespoon chopped fresh coriander leaves

1 tablespoon lemon juice

Coat fish with cooking-oil spray; barbecue or grill fish until browned both sides and cooked through. Serve fish with Chilli Avocado Salsa.
Chilli Avocado Salsa Combine all ingredients in bowl; mix well.

Per serve fat 14.6g; fibre 2.2g; kj 1362

8 spicy seafood
bouillabaisse

500g boneless white fish fillets

15 (375g) medium uncooked prawns

16 small mussels

1/2 teaspoon olive oil

4 small (520g) tomatoes, peeled, chopped roughly

1 large (300g) red onion, sliced

2 cloves garlic, crushed

2 small fresh red chillies, chopped finely

1/3 cup (65g) basmati rice

10cm strip orange rind

2 cups (500ml) fish stock

2 cups (500ml) water

1 cup (250ml) dry white wine

pinch ground saffron

1 tablespoon chopped fresh dill

Cut fish into 5cm pieces. Shell and devein prawns, leaving heads and tails intact. Scrub mussels; remove beards.

Heat oil in large pan; cook tomato, onion, garlic and chilli, stirring, about 5 minutes or until onion is soft.

Add rice, rind, stock, water, wine and saffron, boil, uncovered, about 10 minutes or until rice is tender, stirring occasionally. Add fish and prawns, simmer, uncovered, about 3 minutes or until seafood is almost tender. Add mussels and dill; cook, covered, about 2 minutes or until mussels open. Discard orange rind.

Microwave Suitable
Per serve fat 5.4g; fibre 3.3g; kj 1474

10 coriander garlic
prawns and noodles

1kg thick fresh rice noodles

2 tablespoons water

1 medium (150g) onion, sliced

4 cloves garlic, crushed

30 (750g) medium uncooked prawns, shelled, halved

3 green onions, chopped

1½ cups (120g) bean sprouts

½ cup fresh coriander leaves

2 small (260g) tomatoes, peeled, seeded, chopped

2 tablespoons finely chopped unsalted roasted peanuts

Place noodles in large bowl, cover with warm water, stand 5 minutes; drain.

Heat water in large non-stick pan; cook onion and garlic, stirring, until onion is soft. Add prawns; cook, stirring, about 3 minutes or until prawns are tender. Stir in green onion and sprouts; cool 10 minutes.

Top noodles with prawn mixture, coriander, tomato and peanuts; drizzle with Dressing. Serve warm or cold.

Dressing Shake ingredients together in jar.

Per serve fat 4.9g; fibre 4.8g; kj 1718

dressing

¼ cup (60ml) lime juice

¼ cup (60ml) fish sauce

1 small fresh red chilli, seeded, chopped finely

1 teaspoon sugar

fish and spinach
cannelloni

250g packet frozen spinach, thawed

15g butter

1 small (80g) onion, chopped finely

1½ tablespoons plain flour

1½ cups (375ml) skim milk

375g boneless white fish fillets, chopped finely

120g packet instant cannelloni tubes

½ cup (60g) grated low-fat cheddar cheese

2 tablespoons grated parmesan cheese

tomato sauce

2 tablespoons water

1 clove garlic, crushed

1 small (80g) onion, chopped finely

1½ cups (375ml) bottled tomato pasta sauce

1 tablespoon chopped fresh basil leaves

Press as much liquid as possible from spinach. Melt butter in medium pan; cook onion, stirring, until soft. Stir in flour; cook over heat until mixture is dry and grainy. Remove from heat, gradually stir in milk. Stir over heat until mixture boils and thickens. Add fish and spinach; simmer, uncovered, 10 minutes; cool.

Place fish mixture into large piping bag without a tube, pipe mixture into cannelloni tubes. Place cannelloni in single layer, in shallow, 2-litre (8-cup) ovenproof dish. Pour Tomato Sauce over cannelloni; sprinkle with combined cheeses. Bake, uncovered, in moderate oven about 40 minutes or until browned.

Tomato Sauce Combine water, garlic and onion in pan; cook, stirring, until onion is soft. Add sauce and basil; simmer, uncovered, about 5 minutes or until thickened slightly.

Per serve fat 9.3g; fibre 6g; kj 1672

12 fish parcels with

lemon ginger dressing

1/4 cup (40g) burghul

16 (400g) medium uncooked prawns

1 small (150g) red capsicum, chopped finely

2 tablespoon chopped fresh chives

cooking-oil spray

4 (600g) ocean perch fillets

lemon ginger dressing
2 tablespoons lemon juice

1 teaspoon grated fresh ginger

2 teaspoons chopped fresh dill

1/4 teaspoon Sichuan pepper

Place burghul in heatproof bowl, cover with boiling water, stand 15 minutes; drain, rinse under cold water, pat dry with absorbent paper.

Shell and devein 8 prawns, leaving tails intact. Shell, devein and chop remaining prawns.

Combine burghul, chopped prawns, capsicum and chives in bowl; mix well. Cut four x 30cm squares of baking paper or foil, coat squares with cooking-oil spray. Place a fillet on each square, top with burghul mixture and whole prawns, drizzle with Lemon Ginger Dressing. Fold paper over top, seal ends completely, place parcels on oven tray. Bake in moderate oven about 15 minutes; open parcels, bake a further 10 minutes or until fish is tender.

Lemon Ginger Dressing Combine all ingredients in bowl; mix well.

Per serve fat 5.5g; fibre 2g; kj 1068

ocean trout 13

with baby vegetables

500g baby beetroots, trimmed

1 bunch (400g) baby carrots, trimmed

2 small (180g) zucchini, sliced

8 tiny (320g) new potatoes, halved

4 baby (100g) onions

800g side of ocean trout

tarragon lemon sauce

20g butter

1 clove garlic, crushed

1 small (80g) onion, chopped

1 tablespoon plain flour

3/4 cup (180ml) skim milk

1 tablespoon chopped fresh tarragon

1 teaspoon grated lemon rind

1 tablespoon lemon juice

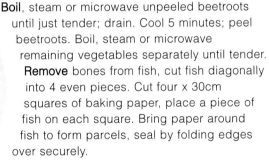

Boil, steam or microwave unpeeled beetroots until just tender; drain. Cool 5 minutes; peel beetroots. Boil, steam or microwave remaining vegetables separately until tender.
Remove bones from fish, cut fish diagonally into 4 even pieces. Cut four x 30cm squares of baking paper, place a piece of fish on each square. Bring paper around fish to form parcels, seal by folding edges over securely.
Place parcels on oven tray, bake in very slow oven about 20 minutes or until fish is tender.
Remove fish from parcels; peel away skin. Serve fish with vegetables and Tarragon Lemon Sauce.
Tarragon Lemon Sauce Heat butter in medium pan; cook garlic and onion, stirring, until onion is soft. Stir in flour; cook over heat until bubbling. Remove from heat, gradually stir in milk. Stir over heat until sauce boils and thickens. Stir in tarragon, rind and juice.

Per serve fat 11g; fibre 9.2g; kj 1440

sauce

You will need to cook about 2 medium (400g) potatoes for this recipe.

415g can red salmon, drained

1 cup mashed potato

2 tablespoons skim milk

1 small (80g) onion, grated

1/2 teaspoon grated lime rind

1 tablespoon chopped fresh chives

1 teaspoon chopped fresh dill

1 egg white

1/4 cup (40g) polenta, approximately

cooking-oil spray

capsicum yogurt sauce

1 medium (200g) red capsicum

1/2 cup (125ml) no-oil herb and garlic dressing

1 teaspoon sugar

1/4 cup (60ml) low-fat yogurt

1 teaspoon chopped fresh dill

Combine salmon, potato, milk, onion, rind, chives, dill and egg white in bowl; mix well. Shape mixture into 8 patties, coat with polenta, place on oven tray which has been coated with cooking-oil spray; refrigerate 30 minutes.

Coat patties with cooking-oil spray. Bake, uncovered, in hot oven about 15 minutes or until browned and hot, turn over halfway through cooking. Serve with Capsicum Yogurt Sauce.

Capsicum Yogurt Sauce
Quarter capsicum, remove seeds and membrane. Roast under grill or in very hot oven, skin side up, until skin blisters and blackens. Cover capsicum pieces in plastic or paper for 5 minutes, peel away skin; chop capsicum. Blend or process capsicum, dressing and sugar until smooth. Add yogurt, process until combined. Stir in dill.

Per serve fat 9.2g; fibre 2.5g; kj 1155

16 chilli ginger octopus
with crisped vegetables

1 medium (120g) carrot

1 small (150g) red capsicum

1.25kg baby octopus

1 tablespoon finely grated fresh ginger

1 tablespoon sweet chilli sauce

1/4 cup (60ml) barbecue sauce

1/2 cup (125ml) orange juice

60g mesclun

Cut carrot into thirds crossways; quarter capsicum, discard seeds. Cut vegetable pieces into thin strips, place in small bowl. Cover with iced water; refrigerate.

Meanwhile, remove and discard heads and beaks from octopus; cut in half. Combine ginger and sauces in medium bowl with octopus, mix well.

Drain octopus over small bowl; reserve sauce mixture. Cook octopus, in batches, in large heated non-stick pan until browned and tender. Cover to keep warm.

Add reserved sauce mixture and juice to same pan. Bring to boil, simmer, uncovered, about 2 minutes or until sauce thickens slightly. Return octopus to pan; stir until glazed and heated through. Serve octopus and sauce with drained crisped vegetables and mesclun.

Per serve fat 2.5g; fibre 2g; kj 844

soup

120g thin dried egg noodles

4 (100g) medium uncooked prawns

4 small mussels

1 litre (4 cups) fish stock

2 stems fresh lemon grass

4 star anise

1 single (170g) chicken breast fillet, sliced

1 small (70g) carrot, sliced

1 baby (150g) bok choy, sliced

2 green onions, sliced

1/2 cup (40g) bean sprouts

1/3 cup chopped fresh coriander leaves

1 teaspoon fish sauce

2 small fresh red chillies, chopped

Add noodles to large pan of boiling water, boil, uncovered, until just tender, rinse under cold water; drain. Shell and devein prawns, leaving tails intact. Scrub mussels, remove beards.

Combine stock, lemon grass and star anise in large pan; bring to boil. Add chicken; simmer, uncovered, until tender, remove from pan. Add prawns and mussels to pan; simmer, uncovered, until prawns are tender and mussels

open, remove from pan.

Strain stock through fine sieve, return stock to pan; discard lemon grass and star anise. Add carrot to pan, simmer, uncovered, 2 minutes. Stir in remaining ingredients; bring to boil. Divide noodles, chicken and seafood between 4 serving bowls; pour over hot stock mixture.

Microwave Suitable
Per serve fat 2.8g; fibre 2.3g; kj 819

18 salmon fillets with
sweet and sour onions

cooking-oil spray

4 (800g) salmon fillets

sweet and sour onions

¹/₃ cup (80ml) water

2 medium (300g) onions, sliced

¹/₃ cup (75g) firmly packed brown sugar

¹/₂ cup (125ml) brown malt vinegar

2 tablespoons raisins

¹/₂ teaspoon grated orange rind

Heat griddle pan, coat with cooking-oil spray; cook salmon fillets until browned both sides and tender. Serve salmon with Sweet and Sour Onions.

Sweet and Sour Onions Combine water and onion in non-stick pan; simmer, covered, stirring occasionally, about 15 minutes or until soft. Add sugar, vinegar and raisins; simmer, uncovered, about 15 minutes or until mixture has thickened, stir in rind.

Microwave Suitable
Per serve fat 9.2g; fibre 1.4g; kj 1664

lemon squid and vegetable stir-fry

800g squid hoods

2 teaspoons fish sauce

1 tablespoon sweet chilli sauce

1 tablespoon soy sauce

2 cloves garlic, crushed

1 teaspoon grated lemon rind

1/4 cup (60ml) lemon juice

2 tablespoons chopped fresh coriander leaves

1 tablespoon honey

2 teaspoons peanut oil

1 medium (150g) onion, sliced

1 medium (120g) carrot, sliced

500g choy sum, chopped

425g can baby corn, rinsed, drained

3 teaspoons cornflour

1/2 cup (125ml) water

1 tablespoon hoi sin sauce

Cut squid hoods open, cut shallow diagonal slashes in criss-cross pattern on inside surface; cut into 2cm x 6cm pieces. Combine sauces, garlic, rind, juice, coriander, honey and squid in medium bowl; mix well. Cover; refrigerate 1 hour.
Remove squid from marinade; reserve marinade. Heat oil in wok or large pan; stir-fry squid, in batches, until just tender, remove from pan. Stir-fry onion and carrot in same pan for 2 minutes.
Add reserved marinade, choy sum and corn; stir-fry until choy sum is just wilted. Add blended cornflour, water and hoi sin sauce, stir over heat until mixture boils and thickens slightly. Return squid to pan; cook, stirring, until hot.

Per serve fat 5.1g; fibre 6.5g; kj 895

20 tuna in spicy

tomato sauce

2 teaspoons olive oil

4 (800g) tuna steaks

spicy tomato sauce

2 tablespoons water

1 small (100g) red onion, chopped

2 cloves garlic, crushed

400g can tomatoes

1 medium (200g) yellow capsicum, chopped finely

1 cup (120g) seeded black olives

1/2 cup (125ml) vegetable stock

1/4 cup (60ml) marsala

2 bay leaves

1 tablespoon chopped fresh oregano

1/2 teaspoon dried crushed chillies

Heat oil in non-stick pan; cook tuna, until browned both sides and tender. Serve with Spicy Tomato Sauce.

Spicy Tomato Sauce Combine water, onion and garlic in pan; cook, stirring, until onion is soft. Add undrained crushed tomatoes and remaining ingredients; simmer, uncovered, about 20 minutes or until thickened slightly. Discard bay leaves.

Per serve fat 9.4g; fibre 3.4g; kj 1344

22 spaghetti with
tuna and capsicum sauce

400g spaghetti

2 tablespoons water

1 medium (200g) green capsicum, sliced thinly

1 medium (150g) onion, sliced

2 x 400g cans tomatoes

2 medium (240g) zucchini, chopped

1 teaspoon sugar

425g can tuna in brine, drained

1/4 cup chopped fresh basil leaves

1/4 cup (20g) grated parmesan cheese

Add pasta to large pan of boiling water, boil, uncovered, until just tender; drain.

Combine water, capsicum and onion in non-stick pan; cook, stirring, until vegetables are tender. Add undrained crushed tomatoes, zucchini and sugar; simmer, uncovered, until zucchini is just tender. Add tuna and basil, stir gently until heated through. Serve sauce over pasta, sprinkle with parmesan.

Microwave Suitable
Per serve fat 5.6g; fibre 9.3g; kj 2241

to go

Shell and devein prawns, leaving tails intact. Remove and discard heads and beaks from octopus; cut in half.
Mix garlic, paprika, 2 tablespoons of the vinegar and paste in medium bowl. Add prawns, octopus and scallops; coat with marinade. Cover; refrigerate at least 3 hours or overnight.
Cook seafood in large heated non-stick pan, until prawns change colour, and both octopus and scallops are tender and cooked as desired.
Meanwhile, quarter pide, cut each piece in half horizontally. Toast pide pieces both sides. Gently toss remaining vinegar with oil and rocket in large bowl; top toasted bread pieces with rocket and seafood just before serving.

Per serve fat 6.5g; fibre 4.1g; kj 1770

20 (500g) medium uncooked prawns

400g baby octopus

2 cloves garlic, crushed

1/2 teaspoon ground sweet paprika

1/4 cup (60ml) balsamic vinegar

2 tablespoons tomato paste

300g scallops

1 long loaf Turkish pide

2 teaspoons olive oil

250g rocket, trimmed

24 teriyaki

fish with noodles

²/₃ cup (160ml) bottled teriyaki marinade

1 clove garlic, crushed

4 (800g) white fish fillets

2 small (300g) red capsicums

4 baby (600g) bok choy, halved

200g Hokkien noodles

2 tablespoons water

Combine marinade with garlic in shallow dish; add fish, turn to coat fish evenly. Cover; refrigerate 1 hour. Quarter capsicums, remove seeds and membranes. Roast under grill or in very hot oven, skin side up, until skin blisters and blackens. Cover capsicum pieces in plastic or paper for 5 minutes, peel away skin.
Boil, steam or microwave bok choy until just tender; drain, cover to keep warm. Pour boiling water over noodles in large heatproof bowl; separate noodles with fork; drain.
Drain fish from marinade; reserve marinade. Add fish to heated non-stick pan; cook until well browned both sides and cooked through; remove from pan. Bring reserved marinade and water to boil in same pan; add noodles, stir until heated through.
Serve fish with noodle mixture, capsicum and baby bok choy.

Per serve fat 6.4g; fibre 5.6g; kj 1488

26 spicy rice
and salmon squares

You will need to cook about 1½ cups (300g) white long-grain rice for this recipe.

415g can red salmon, drained

4 cups cooked white rice

pinch chilli powder

3 egg whites

¼ cup chopped fresh parsley

2 cloves garlic, crushed

2 green onions, chopped

2 tablespoons soy sauce

yogurt dressing

1 cup (250ml) low-fat yogurt

2 tablespoons chopped fresh mint

Line base and sides of 23cm square cake pan with baking paper. Combine all ingredients in bowl; mix well. Spread mixture evenly into prepared pan. Bake, uncovered, in moderate oven about 35 minutes or until firm. Cut into squares, serve with Yogurt Dressing.

Yogurt Dressing Combine yogurt and mint in bowl; mix well.

Per serve fat 10.6g; fibre 2.2g; kj 2001

stir-fried noodles

with chilli prawns

600g Hokkien noodles

15 (750g) large uncooked prawns

1 teaspoon peanut oil

500g baby bok choy

2 tablespoons sweet chilli sauce

¼ cup (60ml) chicken stock

2 tablespoons lime juice

1 clove garlic, crushed

Pour boiling water over noodles in large heatproof bowl; separate noodles with fork, drain. Shell and devein prawns, leaving tails intact.
Heat oil in wok or large pan; stir-fry prawns until just changed in colour. Add noodles, bok choy and combined remaining ingredients; stir-fry until bok choy just wilts and prawns are cooked through.

Per serve fat 4.7g; fibre 10.7g; kj 1370

28 squid in tomato
wine sauce

You will need to cook about 1 cup (200g) white long-grain rice for this recipe.

12 small (1.8kg) squid

2 x 400g cans tomatoes

1 cup (250ml) water

¾ cup (180ml) dry red wine

2 tablespoons tomato paste

2 tablespoons drained capers

1 clove garlic, crushed

2 tablespoons chopped fresh parsley

filling

1 tablespoon water

1 small (80g) onion, chopped finely

2 medium (240g) zucchini, grated

1 clove garlic, crushed

3 cups cooked white rice

⅓ cup (50g) pine nuts, toasted

1 egg, beaten lightly

1 tablespoon chopped fresh basil leaves

2 teaspoons balsamic vinegar

Gently pull head and entrails from squid. Remove and discard clear backbone (quill) from inside body. Firmly pull skin from squid with salted fingers. Remove and discard flaps. Wash and dry hoods, fill hoods with Filling, secure ends with toothpicks.

Combine undrained crushed tomatoes, water, wine, paste, capers and garlic in 3 litre (12-cup) flameproof dish, bring to boil; simmer, uncovered, 10 minutes. Stir in parsley, then add squid in single layer. Bake, covered, in moderate oven about 1 hour or until squid is tender.

Filling Combine water, onion, zucchini and garlic in non-stick pan; cook, stirring, until onion is soft. Remove from heat and stir in remaining ingredients.

Per serve fat 13.2g; fibre 6.1g; kj 2181

ginger

chilli crab

Place live crabs in freezer for at least 2 hours; this is the most humane way of killing a crab. Slide a sharp strong knife under top shell at back of crabs, lever off shell and discard.

Remove and discard gills, wash crabs thoroughly. Chop body into quarters with cleaver. Remove claws and nippers, chop or break nippers into large pieces.

Heat oil in wok or large pan; cook onion, ginger, garlic and chilli, stirring, until fragrant. Add vinegar, stock, sugar and sauce, bring to boil, stir in blended cornflour and water, stir over heat until mixture boils and thickens. Add crab; cook, covered, 15 minutes, stirring occasionally.

Per serve fat 6g; fibre 0.7g; kj 960

2 x 1.5kg uncooked mud crabs

2 teaspoons peanut oil

4 green onions, chopped

2 tablespoons grated fresh ginger

3 cloves garlic, crushed

3 small fresh red chillies, chopped

2 tablespoons rice vinegar

3/4 cup (180ml) fish stock

1 tablespoon palm sugar

1 tablespoon soy sauce

1 teaspoon cornflour

2 teaspoons water

30 cajun fish cutlets

with cannellini bean salad

We used blue eye cutlets for this recipe.

1 tablespoon Cajun seasoning

1 tablespoon plain flour

1 teaspoon ground cumin

4 (1kg) white fish cutlets

cooking-oil spray

1 x 400g can cannellini beans

1 (130g) Lebanese cucumber, seeded, chopped finely

½ medium (100g) red capsicum, chopped finely

1 small (100g) red onion

2 tablespoons lime juice

Combine seasoning, flour and cumin in small bowl; sprinkle over both sides of fish. Heat griddle pan, coat with cooking-oil spray; cook fish until browned both sides and cooked through.

Meanwhile, combine beans, cucumber, capsicum, onion and lime juice in medium bowl. Serve with fish.

Per serve fat 7.4g; fibre 6.5g; kj 1323

shredded crab

salad

We used fresh cooked crab meat for this recipe.

50g bean thread vermicelli noodles

500g cooked crab meat

500g radishes, trimmed, sliced thinly

100g snow pea sprouts

2 green onions, chopped

dressing

1/3 cup (80ml) lime juice

1/3 cup chopped fresh coriander leaves

1 tablespoon sweet chilli sauce

1 tablespoon fish sauce

3 teaspoons sambal oelek

Place noodles in heatproof bowl, cover with boiling water, stand 5 minutes, drain; chop. Squeeze excess moisture from crab meat. Combine noodles, crab meat, radish, sprouts and onion in a bowl. Just before serving, drizzle with Dressing; mix gently.
Dressing Combine all ingredients in jar; shake well.

Per serve fat 1.4g; fibre 2.5g; kj 652

quick prawns

salt and pepper prawns

*1kg medium
uncooked prawns*

2 cloves garlic, crushed

*1 small fresh red chilli,
sliced thinly*

1 tablespoon lime juice

2 tablespoons sweet chilli sauce

1/2 teaspoon ground black pepper

1/2 teaspoon sea salt flakes

3 green onions, sliced thinly

*2 teaspoons sesame
seeds, toasted*

garlic prawns

1kg medium uncooked prawns

1 teaspoon olive oil

*1 medium (170g) red onion,
chopped*

3 cloves garlic, crushed

1/4 cup (60ml) dry white wine

2 x 400g cans tomatoes

2 tablespoons tomato paste

1 teaspoon sugar

*2 tablespoons chopped fresh
parsley*

Shell and devein prawns, leaving
tails intact. Heat oil in large pan;
cook onion and garlic, stirring,
until onion is soft. Add wine,
undrained crushed tomatoes,
paste, sugar and half the parsley;
simmer, uncovered, 5 minutes or
until sauce thickens slightly. Add
prawns; cook, stirring, until pink.
Sprinkle with remaining parsley.

Per serve fat 3.6g; fibre 3.9g; kj 845

Shell and
devein
prawns,
leaving
tails
intact.
Cook
prawns, in
batches, in large
heated non-stick pan,
stirring, until changed in colour.
Return prawns to pan with garlic
and chilli; cook, stirring for
1 minute, until fragrant. Add
juice, sauce, pepper and salt;
cook, stirring, until heated
through. Serve sprinkled with
onion and seeds.

Per serve fat 2.2g; fibre 1g; kj576

thai-style prawns

1kg medium uncooked prawns
1 tablespoon red curry paste
1 tablespoon fish sauce
2 tablespoons lime juice
2 tablespoons soy sauce
1 medium (200g) red capsicum, sliced thinly
200g baby spinach leaves
2 tablespoons chopped fresh coriander leaves

Shell and devein prawns, leaving tails intact. Mix prawns with curry paste, and cook in batches, in large heated non-stick pan, stirring until prawns are just tender. Return prawns to pan with remaining ingredients. Cook, stirring, until spinach is wilted.
Per serve fat 2.1g; fibre 1.9g; kj 632

honey prawns

1kg medium uncooked prawns
cooking-oil spray
2 cloves garlic, crushed
1 tablespoon grated fresh ginger
1/2 cup (125ml) honey
1 cup (250ml) chicken stock
3 teaspoons cornflour
1/4 cup salt-reduced soy sauce

Shell and devein prawns, leaving tails intact. Cook prawns, in batches, on heated griddle which has been coated with cooking-oil spray, until changed in colour and tender. Remove from pan, cover to keep warm.
Cook garlic and ginger in pan, stirring, until fragrant. Add honey and stock, stir in blended cornflour and sauce; stir over heat until sauce boils and thickens. Serve over prawns.
Per serve fat 1.6g; fibre 0.3g; kj 979

34 fish and vegetable
kebabs

soak bamboo skewers in water for 1 hour to prevent burning.

3 (600g) white fish fillets

3 medium (360g) zucchini

12 baby (150g) yellow squash

1 medium (200g) red capsicum, chopped roughly

¼ cup (60ml) soy sauce

½ teaspoon sesame oil

1½ tablespoons honey

2 tablespoons dry sherry

¼ cup (60ml) lemon juice

1 clove garlic, crushed

Cut fish into 3cm cubes. Cut zucchini into 2cm slices. Boil, steam or microwave zucchini and squash until just tender.
Thread fish, zucchini, squash and capsicum onto 12 skewers. Place kebabs in large dish, pour over combined remaining ingredients, turn kebabs to coat. Cover; refrigerate at least 3 hours or overnight. Drain kebabs; reserve the marinade.
Grill kebabs until fish is cooked through, brushing often with reserved marinade.

Per serve fat 5.3g; fibre 3g; kj 1047

36 grilled lobster soup

2 medium (800g) uncooked
lobster tails

1 medium (120g) carrot

1 small (150g) red capsicum

1 small (150g) yellow capsicum

100g snow peas

2 litres (8 cups) fish stock

1 small fresh red chilli, chopped
finely

1 tablespoon grated fresh ginger

1/4 cup lightly packed fresh
coriander leaves

Remove shells from lobster tails,
cut lobster meat in half lengthways,
grill until tender. Cut lobster into
slices. Cut carrot, capsicum and
snow peas into thin strips. Heat
fish stock in large pan until hot.
Divide lobster, vegetables, chilli,
ginger and coriander between
serving bowls; pour over hot stock.

Per serve fat 2.3g; fibre 2.2g; kj 807

pesto fish

with hot tomato salsa

We used whiting fillets for this recipe.

12 small (500g) white fish fillets

2 tablespoons bottled pesto

2 tablespoons water

1 large (350g) green capsicum, chopped

4 medium (300g) egg tomatoes, chopped

²/₃ cup (100g) black olives

Brush fish with pesto. Combine water and capsicum in small pan; cook, stirring, until just soft. Add tomato and olives; cook, stirring, until tomato is soft.

Meanwhile, heat large non-stick pan; cook fish, in batches, until browned lightly both sides and cooked through. Serve fish with tomato and capsicum mixture.

Per serve fat 10.7g; fibre 2.7g; kj 908

38 thai-style

stir-fried prawn salad

20 (500g) medium uncooked prawns

1 clove garlic, crushed

2 tablespoons lime juice

1 tablespoon sweet chilli sauce

1½ teaspoons fish sauce

1 tablespoon chopped fresh coriander leaves

1 tablespoon chopped fresh lemon grass

250g asparagus

2 teaspoons peanut oil

500g baby bok choy, chopped

1 medium (200g) yellow capsicum, chopped

80g snow pea sprouts

1 tablespoon shredded fresh basil leaves

Shell and devein prawns, leaving tails intact. Combine prawns, garlic, 1 tablespoon of the juice, chilli sauce, ½ teaspoon of the fish sauce, coriander and lemon grass in bowl; mix well. Cover; refrigerate 3 hours or overnight.

Drain prawns; discard marinade. Cut asparagus into 5cm lengths. Add asparagus to large pan of boiling water, drain immediately, rinse under cold water; drain.

Heat oil in wok or large pan; stir-fry prawns until tender, remove from pan. Add asparagus, bok choy and capsicum to pan; stir-fry until bok choy is wilted. Add remaining juice, remaining fish sauce, sprouts and basil; stir-fry until sprouts are just wilted. Serve vegetables topped with prawns.

Per serve fat 3.3g; fibre 3.5g; kj 504

40 tarragon fish and
vegetable parcels

We used blue eye fillets for this recipe.

1 medium (350g) leek

1 large (180g) carrot

cooking-oil spray

2 tablespoons dry white wine

2 teaspoons chopped fresh tarragon leaves

4 (800g) white fish fillets

Cut leek and carrot into thin 4cm-long strips. Heat large non-stick pan, coat with cooking-oil spray; cook vegetables, stirring, until softened slightly. Stir in wine and tarragon; cook, uncovered, 1 minute.

Place each fish fillet on a 30cm-square piece of foil; divide vegetables among fillets. Wrap tightly to enclose fillets, place on oven tray; bake in hot oven 20 minutes.

Per serve fat 5.4g; fibre 2.7g; kj 884

fish and chips 41

with tartare sauce

6 medium (1.2kg) potatoes

1 egg white

1 teaspoon Lemon Pepper Seasoning

2 cups (140g) stale breadcrumbs

½ teaspoon Lemon Pepper Seasoning, extra

2 teaspoons chopped fresh lemon thyme

⅓ cup (25g) grated parmesan cheese

4 (800g) white fish fillets

1 egg white, beaten lightly, extra

tartare sauce

½ cup (125ml) low-fat yogurt

2 tablespoons drained, chopped gherkins

5 drained capers, chopped

Cut potatoes into thick chips. Boil, steam or microwave chips until just tender, drain; pat dry with absorbent paper. Combine egg white and seasoning in bowl; add chips, stir until well coated. Place chips on baking paper-covered oven tray. Bake, uncovered, in very hot oven about 30 minutes or until browned.

Meanwhile, combine breadcrumbs, extra seasoning, thyme and parmesan in bowl; mix well. Dip fish fillets in extra egg white, press on breadcrumb mixture. Grill fish until browned lightly on both sides and just cooked through. Serve fish and chips with Tartare Sauce.

Tartare Sauce Combine all ingredients in bowl; mix well.

Per serve fat 8.8g; fibre 5.1g; kj 2220

42 fish kofta

700g boneless white fish fillets, chopped

2 medium (300g) onions, chopped

1/2 cup firmly packed fresh coriander leaves

2 large fresh red chillies, chopped

1 tablespoon ghee

2 cloves garlic, crushed

2 teaspoons ground coriander

1 teaspoon ground cumin

1/2 teaspoon ground turmeric

2 cinnamon sticks

1 teaspoon ground fenugreek

3 medium (570g) tomatoes, peeled, chopped

Bring a large pan of water to boil; add fish, immediately reduce heat, then simmer, uncovered, until fish is just tender. Strain fish over large bowl; reserve 2 cups (500ml) liquid.

Blend or process fish with half the onion, half the fresh coriander and all the chilli until just combined. Shape rounded tablespoons of mixture into sausage shapes (kofta), place on tray; refrigerate 30 minutes.

Heat half the ghee in non-stick pan; cook kofta, in batches, until browned both sides; drain on absorbent paper. Heat remaining ghee in a large pan; cook remaining half onion, garlic and all spices, stirring, until onion is browned lightly. Add tomato; cook, stirring, about 5 minutes or until tomato is very soft. Add reserved liquid; simmer, uncovered, about 10 minutes or until sauce is thickened.

Add kofta; simmer, uncovered, 5 minutes or until kofta are heated through. Just before serving, sprinkle with remaining coriander leaves.

Per serve fat 10.5g; fibre 4g; kj 1180

44 spicy tomato
coriander prawns

40 (1kg) medium uncooked prawns

2 teaspoons hot paprika

1 teaspoon coriander seeds, crushed

1 teaspoon ground turmeric

1 teaspoon ground cumin

1 teaspoon cracked black pepper

1/4 teaspoon ground cloves

1/4 teaspoon ground cardamom

1/4 cup (60ml) water

1 tablespoon water, extra

2 medium (300g) onions, sliced

2 large (500g) tomatoes, chopped

2 tablespoons finely shredded fresh coriander leaves

Shell and devein prawns, leaving tails intact. Combine spices and water in small bowl; mix well. Heat extra water in non-stick pan; cook onion, stirring, 2 minutes. Add spice mixture; cook, stirring, until fragrant. Add prawns and tomato; cook, stirring, until prawns are just tender. Remove from heat; stir in fresh coriander.

Microwave Suitable

Per serve fat 1.4g; fibre 3.6g; kj 657

snapper with a
triple-cheese crust

1 tablespoon Dijon mustard

1 cup (70g) stale breadcrumbs

1/3 cup (35g) coarsely grated
low-fat mozzarella cheese

1/3 cup (40g) coarsely grated
low-fat cheddar cheese

1/3 cup (25g) coarsely grated
parmesan cheese

2 tablespoons finely chopped
fresh parsley

2 cloves garlic, crushed

2 teaspoons Lemon Pepper
Seasoning

4 (800g) snapper fillets

cooking-oil spray

Combine mustard,
breadcrumbs, cheeses,
parsley, garlic and Seasoning
in large bowl.

Place fish on oven tray which
has been coated with cooking-
oil spray. Press cheese
mixture onto fish; coat with
cooking-oil spray.

Bake, uncovered, in hot oven
about 15 minutes or until
cheese browns and fish is
cooked through.

Per serve fat 8.8g; fibre 1g; kj 2079

46 thai-style fish
and corn cakes

You will need to cook about 1/3 cup (65g) rice for this recipe.

750g redfish fillets

1 tablespoon grated fresh ginger

1 large fresh red chilli, seeded, chopped

2 cloves garlic, peeled

2 green onions, chopped

1/4 cup fresh coriander leaves

2 teaspoons grated lime rind

1 tablespoon fish sauce

1 egg

1 cup cooked jasmine rice

310g can corn kernels, drained

2 teaspoons peanut oil

pineapple salsa

1/2 small (400g) fresh pineapple, chopped finely

2 teaspoons grated lime rind

1 large fresh red chilli, seeded, chopped finely

Process fish, ginger, chilli, garlic, onion, coriander, rind, sauce and egg until well combined. Transfer fish mixture to large bowl, stir in rice and corn.

Roll mixture into 16 balls, flatten slightly. Heat oil in large non-stick pan; cook fish cakes, in batches, until browned both sides and cooked through. Serve with Pineapple Salsa.

Pineapple Salsa Combine all ingredients in bowl; mix well.

Freeze Uncooked fish cakes suitable
Per serve fat 9.7g; fibre 4.2g; kj 1632

polenta-coated fish
with lentil salsa

We used whiting fillets for this recipe.

8 small (800g) white fish fillets

plain flour

1 egg, beaten lightly

1 tablespoon skim milk

1 cup (170g) polenta

2 teaspoons olive oil

lentil salsa

1 cup (200g) red lentils, rinsed, drained

2 medium (400g) red capsicums

1 medium (200g) yellow capsicum

1/4 cup chopped fresh mint leaves

2 tablespoons chopped fresh parsley

dressing

1/4 cup (60ml) lemon juice

2 teaspoons olive oil

2 tablespoons sweet chilli sauce

Toss fish in flour, shake away excess flour. Dip fish in combined egg and milk, then in polenta. Heat oil in large non-stick pan; cook fish, in batches, until browned lightly all over and cooked through. Serve fish with Lentil Salsa; drizzled with remaining Dressing.

Lentil Salsa Add lentils to medium pan of boiling water, boil, uncovered, about 5 minutes or until just tender; drain. Quarter capsicums, remove seeds and membranes. Roast under grill or in very hot oven, skin side up, until skin blisters and blackens. Cover capsicum pieces in plastic or paper for 5 minutes, peel away skin. Chop capsicum finely. Combine lentils, capsicum, herbs and half the Dressing in bowl; mix well.

Dressing Combine all ingredients in screw-top jar; shake well.

Per serve fat 14.1g; fibre 10.4g; kj 2666

48 tortellini and

smoked salmon salad

500g cheese and spinach tortellini

200g sliced smoked salmon

1 tablespoon drained capers

1 tablespoon chopped fresh dill

100g mesclun

dill yogurt dressing

1/4 cup (60ml) low-fat yogurt

2 tablespoons chopped fresh dill

1 tablespoon honey

2 teaspoons Dijon mustard

1 clove garlic, crushed

2 teaspoons lemon juice

Add tortellini to large pan of boiling water, boil, uncovered, until just tender; drain. Cut salmon into strips lengthways, roll up. Combine tortellini, salmon rolls, capers and dill in large bowl, add Dill Yogurt Dressing; mix gently. Serve tortellini mixture over mesclun.
Dill Yogurt Dressing Combine all ingredients in bowl; mix well.

Microwave Tortellini suitable
Per serve fat 8.6g; fibre 5.3g; kj 1070

prawn, cabbage

and rice stir-fry

You will need to cook about ⅓ cup (65g) white long-grain rice for this recipe.

2 teaspoons peanut oil

1 clove garlic, crushed

1 small fresh red chilli, chopped finely

4 green onions, chopped

1 medium (200g) red capsicum, chopped

2 sticks celery, chopped

1 cup cooked white rice

2 cups (160g) shredded cabbage

15 (750g) large cooked prawns, shelled

2 tablespoons soy sauce

Heat oil in wok or large pan, stir-fry garlic, chilli, onion, capsicum and celery until celery is just tender. Add rice, cabbage, prawns and sauce; stir-fry until heated through.

Per serve fat 3.2g; fibre 3.3g; kj 796

50 warm chilli
seafood salad

500g penne

2 teaspoons olive oil

750g baby octopus

500g large mussels

20 (500g) medium
uncooked prawns,
shelled

5 large (1.2kg)
tomatoes, peeled,
chopped

2 cloves garlic, crushed

2 small fresh red chillies,
chopped

1½ tablespoons drained capers

¼ cup chopped fresh flat-leaf
parsley

¼ cup (30g) seeded black
olives, sliced

Add pasta to large pan of boiling water, boil, uncovered, until just tender;
drain. Rinse pasta under cold water, drain. Combine pasta with half the oil
in large bowl; toss gently.

Remove and discard heads and beaks from octopus; cut into quarters.
Scrub mussels; remove beards.

Heat remaining oil in large non-stick pan; cook octopus and prawns, in
batches, until just tender, remove from pan. Add mussels to same pan;
cook, covered, until shells open.

Combine seafood with pasta and remaining ingredients in bowl; toss gently
to combine.

Per serve fat 7.9g; fibre 10.5g; kj 2782

octopus
stir-fry

1.25kg baby octopus

1 teaspoon caster sugar

1 clove garlic, crushed

2 teaspoons grated fresh ginger

1/2 teaspoon cracked black pepper

1/4 teaspoon sesame oil

1/4 cup (60ml) tomato sauce

1 tablespoon soy sauce

1 medium (120g) carrot

2 green onions

2 teaspoons peanut oil

1 tablespoon chopped fresh coriander leaves

Remove and discard heads and beaks from octopus; cut in half. Combine octopus, sugar, garlic, ginger, pepper, sesame oil and sauces in bowl; mix well. Cover; refrigerate 3 hours or overnight. **Using** a vegetable peeler, peel carrot lengthways into thin ribbons; cut onions into 5cm lengths. Heat peanut oil in wok or large pan; stir-fry undrained octopus, in batches, until well browned and just cooked through. Return octopus to pan with carrot and onion; stir-fry until hot. Stir in coriander.

Per serve fat 5.2g; fibre 1.5g; kj 835

52 marinated
herbed fish

2 cloves garlic, crushed

1/4 cup (60ml) lemon juice

1 tablespoon chopped fresh rosemary

2 tablespoons chopped fresh parsley

1/4 teaspoon dried crushed chilli

1 teaspoon sugar

1.5kg snapper

cooking-oil spray

2 tablespoons water

1 medium (350g) leek, sliced

2 cloves garlic, crushed, extra

2 teaspoons chopped fresh thyme

2 teaspoons sugar, extra

6 medium (450g) egg tomatoes, quartered

400g can artichoke hearts in brine, drained, quartered

Combine garlic, juice, herbs, chilli and sugar in small bowl; mix well. Cut 3 shallow slits across fish on both sides; brush with herb mixture. Cover; refrigerate 3 hours or overnight. Place fish on large oven tray which has been coated with cooking-oil spray. Bake, uncovered, in moderately hot oven about 30 minutes or until cooked through.

Meanwhile, combine water, leek, extra garlic and thyme in non-stick pan; cook, stirring, until leek is soft. Add extra sugar, tomato and artichokes, cook, stirring, until heated through. Serve vegetables with fish.

Per serve fat 3.6g; fibre 5.6g; kj 859

54 chilli lime fish with

tomato and onion salsa

We used blue eye cutlets for this recipe.

1 clove garlic, crushed

1 tablespoon finely grated lime rind

2 tablespoons oyster sauce

1/2 cup (125ml) sweet chilli sauce

1/2 cup (125ml) lime juice

4 (1kg) white fish cutlets

2 medium (380g) tomatoes, seeded, chopped finely

1 medium (170g) red onion, chopped finely

Combine garlic, rind, oyster sauce, 1/3 cup each of the chilli sauce and juice in large bowl. Add fish; stir to cover with lime mixture. Cover; refrigerate 15 minutes.

Meanwhile, to make salsa, combine tomato, onion and remaining chilli sauce and juice in small bowl. Cover salsa; refrigerate.

Drain fish, reserve lime mixture. Cook fish in large heated non-stick pan, brushing with reserved lime mixture, until browned both sides and just cooked through. Serve fish topped with salsa.

Per serve fat 6.7g; fibre 3.3g; kj 1238

sweet chilli noodles

with clams and mussels

Soak clams in cold water for 2 hours. Change water twice during soaking. Scrub mussels and remove their beards.

Pour boiling water over noodles in large heatproof bowl, separate noodles with fork; drain.

Heat undrained crushed tomatoes, sauces and noodles in large pan. Add clams, mussels and blended cornflour and juice; stir over heat until mixture boils and thickens. Reduce heat, cover; cook a few minutes more, or until clams and mussels open.

1kg fresh clams

800g small mussels

375g Hokkien noodles

2 x 400g cans tomatoes

1/3 cup (80ml) sweet chilli sauce

1/4 cup (60ml) oyster sauce

1 tablespoon cornflour

2 tablespoons lime juice

Per serve fat 2.5g; fibre 8.6g; kj 1160

56 baked crumbed fish

with parsley caper dressing

4 (800g) white fish fillets

2 tablespoons plain flour

2 egg whites, beaten lightly

1 tablespoon skim milk

1½ cups (105g) stale breadcrumbs

¼ cup (30g) oat bran

¼ cup (40g) polenta

cooking-oil spray

parsley caper dressing

1 small (80g) onion, chopped finely

1 tablespoon drained capers, chopped finely

1 cup (250ml) low-fat yogurt

1 teaspoon sugar

1 clove garlic, crushed

1 tablespoon chopped fresh parsley

Toss fish in flour, shake away excess flour. Dip fish into combined egg whites and milk, then combined breadcrumbs, oat bran and polenta. **Place** fish on oven tray that has been coated with cooking-oil spray. Bake, uncovered, in moderately hot oven about 20 minutes or until browned lightly and cooked through. Serve fish with Parsley Caper Dressing. **Parsley Caper Dressing** Combine all ingredients in bowl; mix well.

Freeze Uncooked crumbed fish suitable
Per serve fat 8g; fibre 2.8g; kj 1741

chilli fish and noodle
stir-fry

200g thin dried egg
noodles

500g boneless white
fish fillets

2 teaspoons
peanut oil

200g snow peas,
halved

1 medium (200g)
red capsicum,
sliced

1 medium (200g)
yellow capsicum,
sliced

1 medium (150g)
onion, chopped

1 tablespoon grated
fresh ginger

2 tablespoons lime
juice

1 tablespoon fish
sauce

1 teaspoon bottled
chopped chilli

1/4 cup (60ml) chicken
stock

Add noodles to large pan of boiling water, boil,
uncovered, until just tender; drain.
Cut fish into 4 cm pieces. Heat half the oil in
non-stick wok or large pan; stir-fry fish, in
batches, until cooked through; remove from
pan. Heat remaining oil in same pan; stir-fry
vegetables until just tender. Return fish to pan
with noodles and combined remaining
ingredients; stir gently until hot.

Per serve fat 6.9g; fibre 4g; kj 1604

2 teaspoons olive oil

1 large (200g) onion, chopped

2 cloves garlic, crushed

400g can tomatoes

¼ cup (60ml) dry red wine

¼ cup (60ml) tomato paste

1 tablespoon brown sugar

1 tablespoon balsamic vinegar

½ cup (125ml) water

1kg marinara seafood mix

2 tablespoons coarsely chopped fresh oregano

Heat oil in large pan; cook onion and garlic, stirring, until onion is soft. Add undrained crushed tomatoes, wine, paste, sugar, vinegar and water. Bring to boil; simmer, uncovered, about 20 minutes or until sauce thickens.

Add marinara mix to tomato sauce; simmer, uncovered, about 10 minutes or until seafood is cooked through. Sprinkle with oregano just before serving.

Per serve fat 6.4g; fibre 2.8g; kj 1319

glossary

barbecue sauce a spicy, tomato-based sauce used to marinate, baste or as an accompaniment.

bean mix (4 bean mix) a canned mix of red kidney, garbanzo, baby lima and butter beans.

breadcrumbs, stale one- or two-day-old bread made into crumbs by grating, blending or processing.

burghul also known as bulgur wheat; hulled steamed and crushed wheat kernels.

butter 125g is equal to 1 stick (4 oz) butter.

cajun seasoning can include paprika, basil, onion, fennel, thyme, cayenne and tarragon.

capsicum also known as bell pepper.

cornflour also known as cornstarch.

eggplant also known as aubergine.

fish sauce also called nam pla or nuoc nam; made from pulverised salted fermented fish.

flour, plain an all-purpose flour, made from wheat.

ghee clarified butter; with the milk solids removed, can be heated to high temperature without burning.

ginger also known as green or root ginger.

hoisin sauce a thick, sweet and spicy Chinese paste made from salted fermented soy beans, onions and garlic.

lemon grass a lemon-smelling and tasting grass; the white lower part of each stem is used.

lemon pepper seasoning crushed black pepper blended with lemon, herbs and spices.

lobster use crayfish.

marinara mix a mixture of uncooked, chopped seafood.

marsala a sweet fortified wine originally from Sicily.

mesclun also known as salad mix; a mixture of assorted young lettuce and other green leaves

mortar and pestle used for grinding, the mortar being the bowl and the pestle the grinding implement. Used widely for spices.

noodles

bean thread vermicelli: also called cellophane; made from green mung bean flour. Good softened in soups and salads or deep-fried with vegetables.

hokkien: also known as stir-fry noodles; fresh wheat flour noodles resembling thick, yellow-brown spaghetti, needing no pre-cooking before being used.

oil

cooking-oil spray: vegetable oil in an aerosol can, available in supermarkets.

olive: a mono-unsaturated oil, especially good for everyday cooking and in salad dressings. "Light" describes the mild flavour, not the fat levels.

peanut: pressed from ground peanuts; often used in Asian cooking because of its high smoke point.

sesame: made from roasted, crushed, white sesame seeds; a flavouring rather than a cooking medium.

onion

green: also known as scallion or (incorrectly)

shallot; an immature onion picked before the bulb has formed, having a long, bright-green edible stalk.

red: also known as Spanish, or Bermuda onion; sweet-flavoured, large and red.

oyster sauce a thick dark-brown sauce made from oysters, salt and soy sauce.

paprika ground dried red capsicum (bell pepper), available sweet or hot.

polenta a flour-like cereal made of ground corn (maize); similar to cornmeal but coarser; also the name of the dish made from it.

rice

arborio: small, round-grained rice which absorbs a large amount of liquid; especially suitable for risotto.

basmati: a white, fragrant long-grained rice. It should be washed several times before cooking.

jasmine: fragrant long-grained rice; white rice can be substituted but will not taste the same.

long-grain: elongated grain, remains separate when cooked; most popular steaming rice in Asia.

rocket also called arugula, rugula or rucola; a peppery-tasting salad green.

scallops a bivalve mollusc with fluted shell valve; we use scallops having the coral (roe) attached.

sichuan pepper also known as Chinese pepper, small, red-brown aromatic seeds with a lemony flavour.

snow peas also called mange tout ("eat all").

squash also known as pattipan, scallopine or summer squash; small, flattish yellow or green-skinned squash.

star anise a dried star-shaped pod with astringent aniseed-flavoured seeds.

sugar, palm very fine sugar from the coconut palm. It is sold in cakes, also known as gula jawa, gula melaka and jaggery. Brown or black sugar can be substituted.

teriyaki marinade a blend of soy sauce, wine, vinegar and spices.

tomato

paste: a concentrated tomato puree.

puree: canned pureed tomatoes (not a concentrate); use fresh, peeled, pureed tomatoes as a substitute.

sauce: also known as ketchup or catsup; a flavoured condiment based on tomatoes, vinegar and spices.

turkish pide (Turkish bread): comes in long (about 45cm) flat loaves as well as individual rounds; made from wheat flour and sprinkled with sesame or black onion seeds.

zucchini also known as courgette.

index

facts and figures 63

These conversions are approximate only, but the difference between an exact and the approximate conversion of various liquid and dry measures is minimal and will not affect your cooking results.

Measuring equipment

The difference between one country's measuring cups and another's is, at most, within a 2 or 3 teaspoon variance. (For the record, 1 Australian metric measuring cup holds approximately 250ml.) The most accurate way of measuring dry ingredients is to weigh them. For liquids, use a clear glass or plastic jug having metric markings.

Note: NZ, Canada, USA and UK all use 15ml tablespoons. Australian tablespoons measure 20ml.
All cup and spoon measurements are level.

How to measure

When using graduated measuring cups, shake dry ingredients loosely into the appropriate cup. Do not tap the cup on a bench or tightly pack the ingredients unless directed to do so. Level the top of measuring cups and measuring spoons with a knife. When measuring liquids, place a clear glass or plastic jug having metric markings on a flat surface to check accuracy at eye level.

Dry Measures

metric	imperial
15g	1/2oz
30g	1oz
60g	2oz
90g	3oz
125g	4oz (1/4lb)
155g	5oz
185g	6oz
220g	7oz
250g	8oz (1/2lb)
280g	9oz
315g	10oz
345g	11oz
375g	12oz (3/4lb)
410g	13oz
440g	14oz
470g	15oz
500g	16oz (1lb)
750g	24oz (11/2lb)
1kg	32oz (2lb)

We use large eggs having an average weight of 60g.

Liquid Measures

metric	imperial
30ml	1 fluid oz
60ml	2 fluid oz
100ml	3 fluid oz
125ml	4 fluid oz
150ml	5 fluid oz (1/4 pint/1 gill)
190ml	6 fluid oz
250ml (1cup)	8 fluid oz
300ml	10 fluid oz (1/2 pint)
500ml	16 fluid oz
600ml	20 fluid oz (1 pint)
1000ml (1litre)	13/4 pints

Helpful Measures

metric	imperial
3mm	1/8in
6mm	1/4in
1cm	1/2in
2cm	3/4in
2.5cm	1in
6cm	21/2in
8cm	3in
20cm	8in
23cm	9in
25cm	10in
30cm	12in (1ft)

Oven Temperatures

These oven temperatures are only a guide.
Always check the manufacturer's manual.

	C°(Celsius)	F°(Fahrenheit)	Gas Mark
Very slow	120	250	1
Slow	150	300	2
Moderately slow	160	325	3
Moderate	180 –190	350 – 375	4
Moderately hot	200 – 210	400 – 425	5
Hot	220 – 230	450 – 475	6
Very hot	240 – 250	500 – 525	7

Food editor Pamela Clark
Associate food editor Karen Hammial
Assistant food editor Kathy McGarry
Assistant recipe editor Elizabeth Hooper
Home Library Staff
Editor-in-chief Mary Coleman
Marketing manager Nicole Pizanis
Editor Susan Tomnay
Subeditor Bianca Martin
Concept design Jackie Richards
Designer Sue de Guingand
Group publisher Paul Dykzeul

Produced by The Australian Women's Weekly Home Library, Sydney.

Colour separations by ACP Colour Graphics Pty Ltd, Sydney.
Printing by Diamond Press Limited, Sydney.

Published by ACP Publishing Pty Limited, 54 Park St, Sydney;
GPO Box 4088, Sydney, NSW 1028. Ph: (02) 9282 8618 Fax: (02) 9267 9438.

AWWHomeLib@publishing.acp.com.au

Australia: Distributed by Network Distribution Company,
GPO Box 4088, Sydney, NSW 1028. Ph: (02) 9282 8777 Fax: (02) 9264 3278.

United Kingdom: Distributed by Australian Consolidated Press (UK),
Moulton Park Business Centre, Red House Rd, Moulton Park, Northampton, NN3 6AQ.

Ph: (01604) 497 531 Fax: (01604) 497 533 Acpukltd@aol.com

Canada: Distributed by Whitecap Books Ltd,
351 Lynn Ave, North Vancouver, BC, V7J 2C4, (604) 980 9852.

New Zealand: Distributed by Netlink Distribution Company,
17B Hargreaves St, Level 5, College Hill, Auckland 1, (9) 302 7616.

South Africa: Distributed by PSD Promotions (Pty) Ltd,
PO Box 1175, Isando 1600, SA, (011) 392 6065.

Healthy Eating: Seafood

Includes index.
ISBN 1 86396 124 0.

1.Cookery (Seafood) I. Title: Australian Women's Weekly.
(Series: Australian Women's Weekly healthy eating mini series).
641.692

ACP Publishing Pty Limited 1999
ACN 053 273 546

Cover: Cajun fish cutlets with cannellini bean salad, page 30.
Stylist Michelle Noerianto **Photographer** Scott Cameron
Plate from Sirocco Homewares, Willoughby

Back cover: Sweet chilli noodles with clams and mussels, page 55